Alpha

wolf

[illegible]